Master Maths at Home

Extra Challenges

Scan the QR code to help your child's learning at home.

How to use this book

Maths — No Problem! created **Master Maths at Home** to help children develop fluency in the subject and a rich understanding of core concepts.

Key features of the Master Maths at Home books include:

- Carefully designed lessons that provide structure, but also allow flexibility in how they're used.

- Speech bubbles containing content designed to spark diverse conversations, with many discussion points that don't have obvious 'right' or 'wrong' answers.

- Rich illustrations that will guide children to a discussion of shapes and units of measurement, allowing them to make connections to the wider world around them.

- Exercises that allow a flexible approach and can be adapted to suit any child's cognitive or functional ability.

- Clearly laid-out pages that encourage children to practise a range of higher-order skills.

- A community of friendly and relatable characters who introduce each lesson and come along as your child progresses through the series.

You can see more guidance on how to use these books at **mastermathsathome.com**.

We're excited to share all the ways you can learn maths!

Copyright © 2022 Maths — No Problem!

Maths — No Problem!
mastermathsathome.com
www.mathsnoproblem.com
hello@mathsnoproblem.com

First published in Great Britain in 2022 by
Dorling Kindersley Limited
One Embassy Gardens, 8 Viaduct Gardens, London SW11 7BW
A Penguin Random House Company

The authorised representative in the EEA is Dorling Kindersley
Verlag GmbH. Amulfstr. 124, 80636 Munich, Germany

10 9 8 7 6 5 4 3 2 1
001–327086–Jan/22

A CIP catalogue record for this book is available from the British Library.

ISBN: 978-0-24153-927-9
Printed and bound in the UK

For the curious
www.dk.com

This book was made with Forest Stewardship Council™ certified paper - one small step in DK's commitment to a sustainable future. For more information go to www. dk.com/our-green-pledge

Acknowledgements
The publisher would like to thank the authors and consultants Andy Psarianos, Judy Hornigold, Adam Gifford and Dr Anne Hermanson.

The Castledown typeface has been used with permission from the Colophon Foundry.

Contents

Ruby   Elliott   Amira   Charles   Lulu   Sam   Oak   Holly   Ravi   Emma   Jacob   Hannah

Making and comparing numbers

Starter

Holly uses these digits to make 3-digit numbers.

What is the greatest 3-digit even number she can make?
What is the greatest 3-digit odd number she can make?
What is the greatest number she can make?

Example

Holly makes these 3-digit even numbers.
368, 386, 638, 836

836 has more hundreds than the other numbers.
The greatest 3-digit even number Holly can make is 836.

Holly makes these 3-digit odd numbers.
683, 863

863 has more hundreds than 683.
863 is the greatest 3-digit odd number Holly can make.

Compare 836 and 863.

836 and 863 have an equal
number of hundreds.
863 has more tens.
863 is the greatest number Holly can make.

Look at the hundreds.

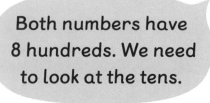

Both numbers have 8 hundreds. We need to look at the tens.

1 | 3 | | 7 | | 4 | | 8 | | 1 |

Use the digits above to make:

(a) the greatest 3-digit even number ☐

(b) the smallest 3-digit even number ☐

(c) the greatest 3-digit odd number ☐

(d) the smallest 3-digit odd number ☐

2 Put the numbers you made in order from smallest to greatest.

☐ , ☐ , ☐ , ☐

3 (a) Use the digits below to make all the possible 3-digit numbers.

| 9 | | 6 | | 3 |

(b) Put the numbers you made in order from greatest to smallest.

Number patterns

How can Sam arrange these numbers to make a pattern?

438

238

738

638

538

338

Example

Sam made this pattern.

238, 338, 438, 538, 638, 738

We add 100 each time.

Each number is 100 more than the number before it.

Ravi used these numbers to make a pattern.

749

699

709

719

729

739

Ravi made this pattern.

749, 739, 729, 719, 709, 699

Each number is 10 less than the number before it.

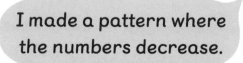

I made a pattern where the numbers decrease.

1 Fill in the blanks to complete the number pattern.

(a) 487, 497, [ ] , [ ] , [ ] , 537

(b) 45, [ ] , [ ] , 345, [ ] , 545

(c) 909, [ ] , 709, [ ] , 509, [ ]

2 Complete the number patterns.

(a) Each number is 10 more than the number before it.

318, [ ] , [ ] , [ ] , [ ] , [ ]

(b) Each number is 10 less than the number before it.

761, [ ] , [ ] , [ ] , [ ] , [ ]

(c) Each number is 100 less than the number before it.

506, [ ] , [ ] , [ ] , [ ] , [ ]

3 Write your own number pattern and complete the sentence to describe it.

[ ] , [ ] , [ ] , [ ] , [ ] , [ ]

Each number is [ ] [ ] than the number before it.

Adding with renaming (part 1)

Starter

Lulu is playing a video game.
She adds 543 bonus points to her score.
What is her score after the bonus points have been added?

543 BONUS POINTS

Score: 398 ♥♥♥

Example

Add 398 and 543.

Step 1   Add the ones.

```
  h   t   o
          1
  3   9   8
+ 5   4   3
_____
          1
```

11 ones = 1 ten + 1 one

8 ones + 3 ones = 11 ones

Step 2   Add the tens.

```
  h   t   o
  1   1
  3   9   8
+ 5   4   3
_____
      4   1
```

14 tens = 1 hundred + 4 tens

1 ten + 9 tens + 4 tens = 14 tens

Step 3   Add the hundreds.

```
    h    t    o
    1    1
    3    9    8
+   5    4    3
─────────────────
    9    4    1
─────────────────
```

1 hundred + 3 hundreds + 5 hundreds = 9 hundreds

Lulu's score is 941.

Practice

1 Add.

(a) 656 + 37 = ☐

(b) 319 + 88 = ☐

(c) 486 + 75 = ☐

(d) 524 + 96 = ☐

2 Add.

(a) 132 + 389 = ☐

(b) 465 + 456 = ☐

(c) 725 + 188 = ☐

(d) 333 + 599 = ☐

Adding with renaming (part 2)

Starter

Ruby walked from her house to the shop.
She then walked from the shop to Emma's house.

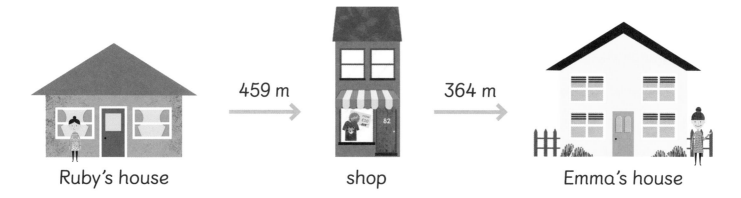

459 m   364 m

Ruby's house   shop   Emma's house

What is the total distance that Ruby walked?

Example

Add 459 and 364.

Step 1   Rename the ones.
          13 ones = 1 ten + 3 ones

```
    h   t   o
            1
    4   5   9
+   3   6   4
_____
            3
_____
```

9 ones + 4 ones = 13 ones

Step 2   Rename the tens.   Step 3   Add the hundreds.
          12 tens = 1 hundred + 2 tens

h	t	o
¹4	¹5	9
+ 3	6	4
	2	3

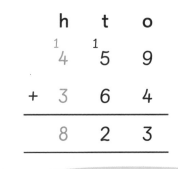

1 ten + 5 tens + 6 tens
= 12 tens

h	t	o
¹4	¹5	9
+ 3	6	4
8	2	3

1 hundred + 4 hundreds
+ 3 hundreds = 8 hundreds

459 + 364 = 823
The total distance Ruby walked is 823 m.

Practice

1   The ground level of a car park can hold 238 cars.
    The first level of the same car park can hold 257 cars.
    How many cars can the car park hold altogether?

    [   ]

    The car park can hold [   ] cars altogether.

2   Sam scored 348 points in a video game.
    Charles scored 293 points in the same game.
    How many points did Sam and Charles score altogether?

    [   ]

    Sam and Charles scored [   ] points altogether.

11

Subtracting with renaming (part 1)

Starter

At the beginning of the year, Class 3 had 300 crayons. At the end of the year, they had only 61 crayons left. How many crayons did Class 3 use?

Example

Subtract 61 from 300.

```
  h   t   o
  2  10
  3   0   0
-     6   1
_____

_____
```

There are not enough ones or tens.

Rename 1 hundred as 10 tens.

```
  h   t   o
  2  9    10
  3  10   0
     0    0
-     6   1
_____
  2   3   9
```

Rename 1 ten as 10 ones.

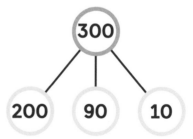

300 – 61 = 239
Class 3 used 239 crayons.

1. A gardener has 400 bulbs to plant. She plants 127 bulbs in one hour. How many bulbs does she have left to plant?

The gardener has [ ] bulbs left to plant.

2. In one day, 375 customers came to a restaurant for either lunch or dinner. There were 286 customers who came to the restaurant for lunch. How many customers came to the restaurant for dinner?

There were [ ] customers who came to the restaurant for dinner.

3. At the school sports day, 410 children took part in races on the field. After the races, 173 children moved from the field to the school hall. The other children stayed on the field. How many children stayed on the field?

[ ] children stayed on the field.

Subtracting with renaming (part 2)

Starter

Sam made a cake and some bread rolls.
He used 615 g of flour to make the cake.
He used 148 g more flour to make the cake
than he used to make the bread rolls.
How many grams of flour did he use to
make the bread rolls?

Example

615 g

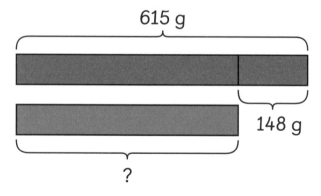

148 g

?

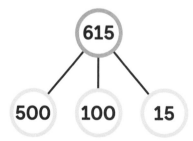

Do we add or subtract?

Subtract 148 from 615.

```
    h    t    o
  5  10ø   15
   ø    1    5
 -  1    4    8
  _____
    4    6    7
  _____
```

615 − 148 = 467

Sam used 467 g of flour to make the bread rolls.

14

1 The distance between Ravi's house and Ruby's house is 563 m.
The distance between Ruby's house and Sam's house is 478 m.
What is the difference between the two distances?

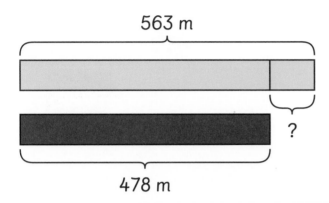

563 m

478 m

?

[ ] – [ ] = [ ]

The difference between the two distances is [ ].

2 The mass of a giraffe is 801 kg. The mass of a water buffalo is 78 kg less than the mass of the giraffe.
What is the mass of the water buffalo?

[ ] – [ ] = [ ]

The mass of the water buffalo is [ ].

Multiplying with renaming

Starter

Each episode of Elliott's favourite programme is 36 minutes long. In one month, Elliott watches 7 episodes. How many minutes of the programme does Elliott watch in one month?

Example

Method 1

```
    h   t   o
        3   6
×           7
    ─────────
        4   2
    2   1   0
    ─────────
    2   5   2
    ─────────
```

Start by multiplying the ones and then multiply the tens.

Method 2

```
    h   t   o
        ⁴
        3   6
×           7
    ─────────
    2   5   2
    ─────────
```

42 ones = 4 tens + 2 ones

36 × 7 = 252

Elliott watches 252 minutes of the programme in one month.

1 There are 7 classrooms in a school. There is 1 box of rulers in each classroom. Each box contains 42 rulers.
How many rulers are in the 7 classrooms altogether?

☐ × ☐ = ☐

There are ☐ rulers in the 7 classrooms altogether.

2 Emma, Ravi and Ruby each buy some packets of stickers.
Each packet contains 24 stickers.
Emma buys 2 packets. Ravi buys twice as many packets as Emma buys.
Ruby buys 1 less packet than Ravi buys.
How many stickers do the children buy altogether?

☐ × ☐ = ☐

The children buy ☐ stickers altogether.

Dividing with renaming

Starter

Seventy-eight children take part in a sports event. The children arrange themselves into teams of 6.
How many teams of 6 children can they make?

Example

Divide 78 by 6.

$$\begin{array}{r} 1 \quad 3 \\ 6\,\overline{)\; 7 \quad {}_{1}8} \end{array}$$

78 = 60 + 18

1 ten + 8 ones = 18

We can make 10 groups of 6 from 60. This leaves 1 ten and 8 ones.

78 ÷ 6 = 13

Divide 18 by 6.
We can make 3 groups of 6.

They can make 13 teams of 6 children.

Practice

1 A teacher shares a bag of tennis balls equally between 5 children.
There are 70 tennis balls in the bag.
How many tennis balls does each child get?

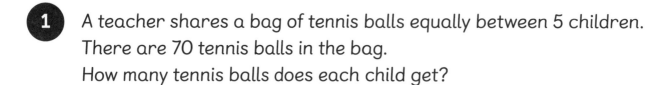

| | ÷ | | = | |

Each child gets ☐ tennis balls.

2 Charles and Sam donate 52 books to the school fair.
They put all of their books into piles of 4.
How many piles of books do they make?

$\boxed{} \div \boxed{} = \boxed{}$

They make $\boxed{}$ piles of books.

3 Ravi, Emma and Holly each have 28 flower seeds.
They plant the seeds in the garden in rows of 6.
How many rows of seeds do the children plant altogether?

$3 \times 28 = \boxed{}$

$\boxed{} \div \boxed{} = \boxed{}$

The children plant $\boxed{}$ rows of seeds altogether.

Multiplication and division

Starter

Charles, Elliott and Hannah count their crayons. They have 95 crayons altogether. Charles has twice as many as Elliott has. Hannah has 5 less than Elliott has.
How many crayons does each of them have?

Example

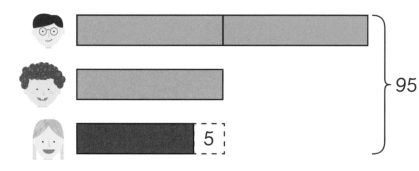

95

If I had 5 more crayons I would have the same number of crayons as Elliott has.

100 ÷ 4 = 25

Charles has 50 crayons, Elliott has 25 crayons and Hannah has 20 crayons.

Practice

1   Emma and Lulu have 48 books between them.
Lulu has 12 more books than Emma has.
How many books does Lulu have?

Lulu has ⬜ books.

2 There are 3 buses taking 100 children to the theatre.
Bus A takes three times as many children as Bus B takes.
Bus C takes 10 more children than Bus B takes.
How many children does each bus take?

Bus A takes

[ ] children.

Bus B takes

[ ] children.

Bus C takes

[ ] children.

3 There are twice as many yellow crayons in a tray as brown crayons.
There are 3 times as many black crayons as brown crayons.
There are 56 yellow crayons.
How many crayons are there altogether?

There are [ ] crayons altogether.

Adding and subtracting fractions

Starter

An oat slice is cut into 6 equal pieces. Ruby takes 2 pieces. Sam takes 3 pieces. What fraction of the oat slice is left?

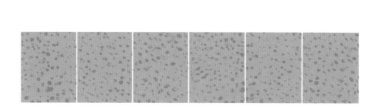

Example

If we cut the oat slice into 6 pieces, each piece is one sixth.

I take $\frac{2}{6}$ of the oat slice.

I take $\frac{3}{6}$ of the oat slice.

$\frac{2}{6} + \frac{3}{6} = \frac{5}{6}$

2 sixths and 3 sixths make 5 sixths.

Altogether, they take $\frac{5}{6}$ of the oat slice.

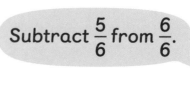
Subtract $\frac{5}{6}$ from $\frac{6}{6}$.

$\frac{1}{6}$ of the oat slice is left.

1 A chocolate bar has 7 equal-sized pieces. Holly takes 2 pieces. Charles takes 2 pieces. What fraction of the chocolate bar is left?

[ ] of the chocolate bar is left.

2 A puzzle is made up of 9 equal parts. Ruby and Elliott complete 2 parts each. Emma completes 1 part.
What fraction of the puzzle hasn't been completed?

[ ] of the puzzle hasn't been completed.

3 A piece of art paper is cut into 10 equal pieces.
Seven children are each given 1 piece.
What fraction of the art paper is left?

[ ] of the art paper is left.

Equivalent fractions

Starter

I take $\frac{1}{4}$ of the cake.

I take $\frac{2}{8}$ of the cake.

Do Jacob and Amira take the same amount of cake?

Example

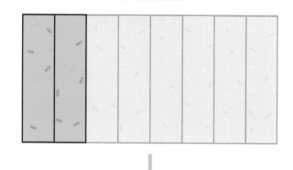

2 eighths is equal to 1 quarter.

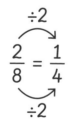

$$\frac{2}{8} = \frac{1}{4}$$

$\div 2$

$\div 2$

When 2 parts become 1 part, 8 parts become 4 parts.

$\frac{2}{8}$ is equivalent to $\frac{1}{4}$. They are equivalent fractions.

$\frac{1}{4}$ is the simplest form of $\frac{2}{8}$.

Jacob and Amira take the same amount of cake.

1 Fill in the blanks to complete the equivalent fractions.

(a) $\frac{3}{9} = \frac{\boxed{}}{3}$

(b) $\frac{6}{10} = \frac{3}{\boxed{}}$

(c) $\frac{8}{12} = \frac{\boxed{}}{36}$

2 Give your answers in the simplest form.

(a) Elliott and Hannah had a whole watermelon.

Elliott took $\frac{1}{6}$ of the watermelon. Hannah took $\frac{3}{6}$ of the watermelon.

How much of the watermelon was left?

$\boxed{}$ of the watermelon was left.

(b) Ruby bought a dozen doughnuts. She and her friends ate $\frac{3}{4}$ of them.

What fraction of the dozen was left?

$\boxed{}$ of the dozen was left.

Comparing fractions

Holly ate $\frac{2}{3}$ of a pizza. Emma ate $\frac{3}{5}$ of a pizza. Who ate more?

Example

1

Holly	$\frac{1}{3}$	$\frac{1}{3}$	$\frac{1}{3}$

Emma	$\frac{1}{5}$	$\frac{1}{5}$	$\frac{1}{5}$	$\frac{1}{5}$	$\frac{1}{5}$

$\frac{2}{3}$ is greater than $\frac{3}{5}$.

$\frac{2}{3}$ is more than $\frac{3}{5}$.

Holly ate more than Emma.

26

1 Compare $\frac{3}{5}$ and $\frac{3}{4}$.

$\frac{3}{5}$

$\frac{3}{4}$

[ ] is greater than [ ] .

2 Compare $\frac{4}{5}$ and $\frac{4}{7}$.

[ ] is less than [ ] .

3 Ravi drank $\frac{1}{3}$ l of milk, Charles drank $\frac{2}{5}$ l of milk and Hannah drank $\frac{3}{8}$ l.

(a) Who drank the most milk? [ ]

(b) Who drank the least? [ ]

Sharing more than 1

Starter

Four 1-litre bottles of orange juice are shared equally between 3 jugs.
How much orange juice is in each jug?

Example

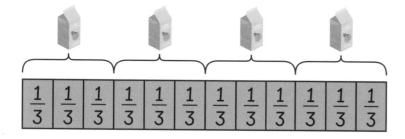

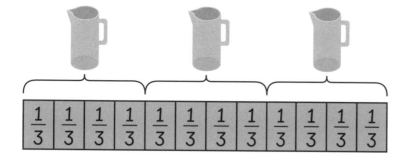

Each jug has $\frac{4}{3}$ l of orange juice.

We write 4 thirds as $\frac{4}{3}$.

28

1 4 children share 5 oranges equally.
How many oranges does each child get?

Each child gets ☐ oranges.

2 5 children share 4 pies equally.
How much pie does each child get?

Each child gets ☐ of a pie.

3 6 friends share 7 bars of chocolate equally.
How much chocolate does each friend get?

Each friend gets ☐ bars of chocolate.

Measuring time

Starter

Ravi and his mum get on a train at 10:45 a.m. They get off the train at 11:20 a.m.

For how many minutes were they on the train?

Example

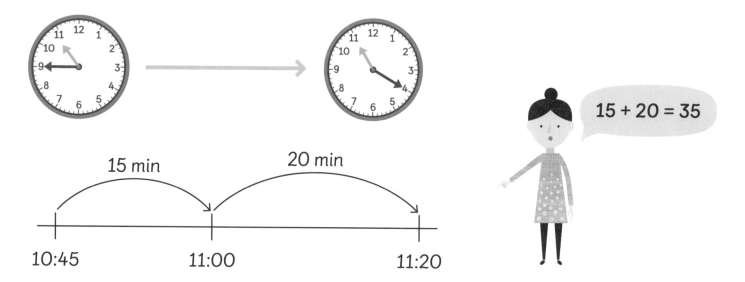

15 + 20 = 35

Ravi and his mum were on the train for 35 minutes.

30

1 Solve and fill in the blanks.

The school bell rings at 10:55 a.m. to start the morning break. It rings again at 11:15 a.m. to end the morning break. How long is the morning break?

10:55   11:00   11:15

☐

☐ + ☐ = ☐

The morning break is ☐ minutes long.

2 Emma started watching a TV programme at 6:52 p.m.
She finished watching the programme at 7:30 p.m.
How long was the programme in minutes?

The programme was ☐ minutes long.

3 Charles started reading his book at 7:43 p.m. He read for 45 minutes.
At what time did Charles stop reading his book?

Charles stopped reading his book at ☐ .

Reading 24-hour clocks

Starter

Holly is attending the boxing class.
At what time does the class start?

Fitness Class Timetable

Time	Studio	Class	
08:35	12		Fast spin
09:55	4		Low spin
13:20	1		Boxing
14:45	3		Side to side
16:30	5		Yoga
17:10	2		Pilates
19:05	7		Strength and stretch

Example

Holly's boxing class starts at   13:20   .

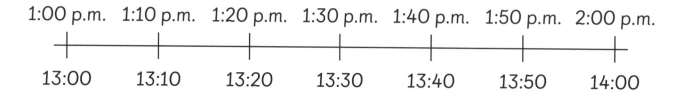

1:00 p.m.   1:10 p.m.   1:20 p.m.   1:30 p.m.   1:40 p.m.   1:50 p.m.   2:00 p.m.

13:00   13:10   13:20   13:30   13:40   13:50   14:00

We can write 13:20 as 1:20 p.m.
We can say 13:20 is 20 minutes past 1 in the afternoon.

Lulu is attending the strength
and stretch class.
At what time does the class start?

19:05   7   Strength and stretch

19:05 is 5 minutes past 7 in the evening.
We can write 19:05 as 7:05 p.m.

Practice

1 Find the start time for each class.

(a) 09:55   4   🌀 Low spin   The class starts at [ ] minutes to

[ ] in the morning.

We can write 09:55 as 9:55 a.m.

(b) 14:45   3   🤸 Side to side   The class starts at [ ] minutes to

[ ] in the [ ].

We can write 14:45 as [ ].

(c) 17:10   2   🛶 Pilates   The class starts at [ ] minutes past

[ ] in the [ ].

We can write 17:10 as [ ].

2 Tell the time shown on the watches.

(a) [ ] minutes past [ ] in the [ ]

10:27   10:27 a.m.

(b) [ ] minutes past [ ] in the [ ]

13:09   [ ]

33

Capacity and volume

Starter

Sam's mum used 12 l of paint to paint 4 walls.
She used an equal amount of paint on each of the walls.
How many litres of paint did she use for each wall?

Example

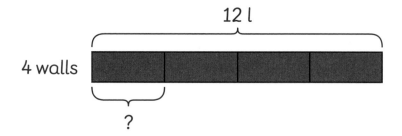

Check.
4 × 3 = 12

12 ÷ 4 = 3

Sam's mum used 3 l of paint for each wall.

Practice

1 Elliott uses 21 l of water a week to water the garden.
He uses the same volume of water each day.
What is the volume of water Elliott uses each day?

[ ]

[ ] ÷ [ ] = [ ]

Elliott uses [ ] of water each day.

2 The volume of juice in a bottle is 3 times the volume of juice in a box.
If the volume of juice in the bottle and the box is 800 ml in total, what is
the volume of juice in the box?

[ ]

The volume of juice in the box is [ ].

3 Oak uses a jug to transfer water into her fish tank. She fills and empties
the jug into the fish tank 5 times in order to fill it. The fish tank holds 15 l of
water. What is the capacity of the jug?

[ ]

The capacity of the the jug is [ ].

Calculating change

Starter

Hannah bought a skateboard and a helmet using three £20 notes. How much change did she receive?

£20 and 15p

£23 and 40p

Example

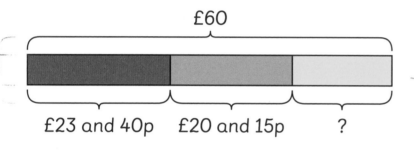

£60

£23 and 40p | £20 and 15p | ?

$3 \times £20 = £60$

Add the pence.
40p + 15p = 55p

Add the pounds.
£23 + £20 = £43

Hannah paid £43 and 55p for the skateboard and the helmet.

£60 − £43 and 55p = £16 and 45p
Hannah received £16 and 45p change.

Subtract £43 and 55p from £60.

Use the pictures to answer the questions.

£18 and 35p £20 and 10p £10 and 20p £15 and 65p

1 Amira bought a cap and a bag with a fifty-pound note.
How much change did she get?

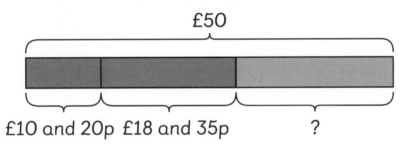

£50

£10 and 20p £18 and 35p ?

Amira got [　　　] change.

2 Sam bought a pair of sunglasses and a pair of shoes. He paid with two £20 notes. How much change did he get?

Sam got [　　　] change.

Calculating amounts of money

The price of a scooter is £124. The price of a bicycle is £240 more than the price of the scooter. The price of a pair of ice skates is £130 less than the bicycle.
What is the price of the bicycle and the ice skates?

Example

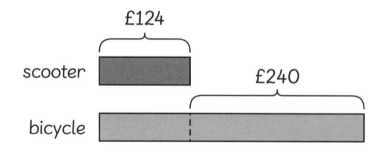

£124

scooter

£240

bicycle

Start by finding the price of the bicycle.

£124 + £240 = £364
The price of the bicycle is £364.

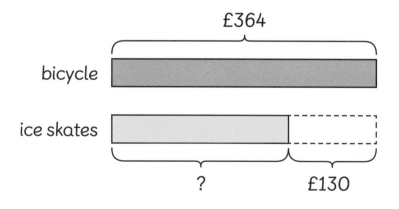

£364

bicycle

ice skates

?   £130

Next, find the price of the ice skates.

£364 − £130 = £234
The price of the ice skates is £234.

1 A hoodie is 4 times the price of a shirt. A pair of gloves is half the price of the hoodie.
If the price of the gloves is £12, what are the prices of the shirt and the hoodie?

shirt
hoodie
gloves

£12

The price of the hoodie is ⬚. The price of the shirt is ⬚.

2 A plumber spends 3 times as much money on materials than a builder spends. An electrician spends twice as much as the plumber spends.
If the plumber, builder and electrician spend £160 altogether, how much does each of them spend?

The builder spends ⬚. The plumber spends ⬚.

The electrician spends ⬚.

Identifying angles

Starter

I can see three different types of angles.

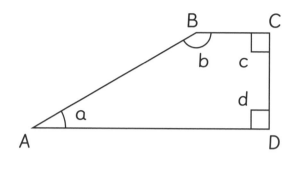

What are the types of angles that Jacob can see?

Example

1

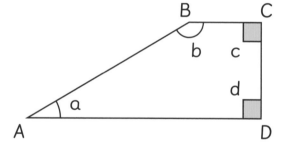

These are right angles.

We can check right angles by using the corner of a book.

2

This is an **acute angle**.

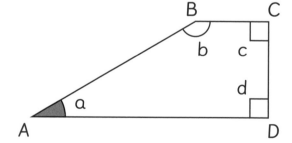

Acute angles are smaller than a right angle.

3

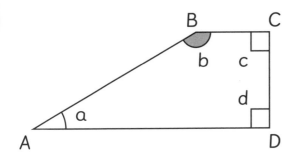

This is an **obtuse angle.**

An obtuse angle is larger than a right angle.
Obtuse angles are never larger than 2 right angles.

Practice

1 Mark the acute, obtuse and right angles on the following quadrilaterals.

Use **a** for acute angles, **o** for obtuse angles and **r** for right angles.
The first one has been done for you.

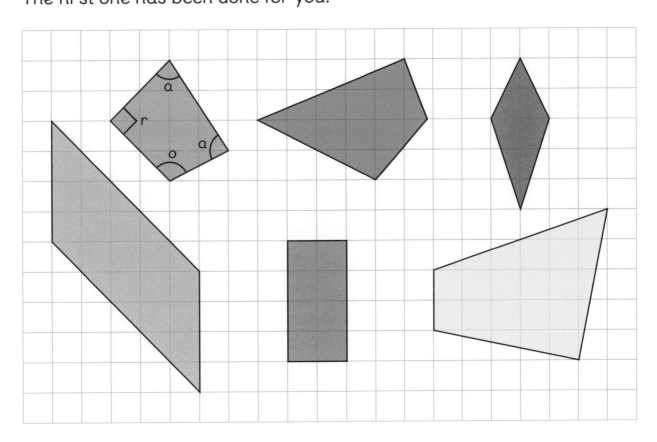

2 (a) Draw a triangle with one right angle.

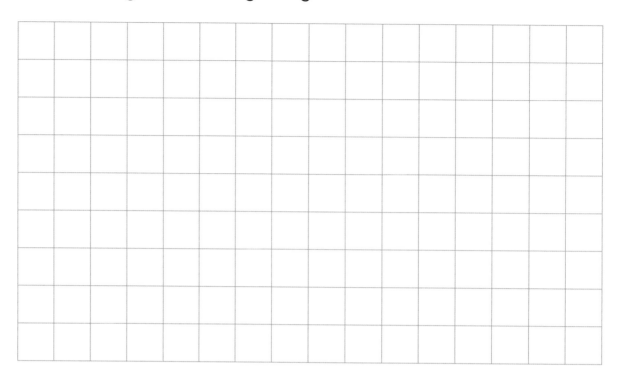

(b) Draw a triangle with one obtuse angle.

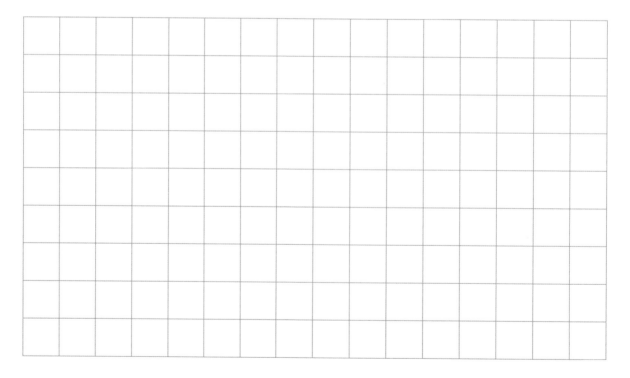

3 Draw a triangle with 3 acute angles.

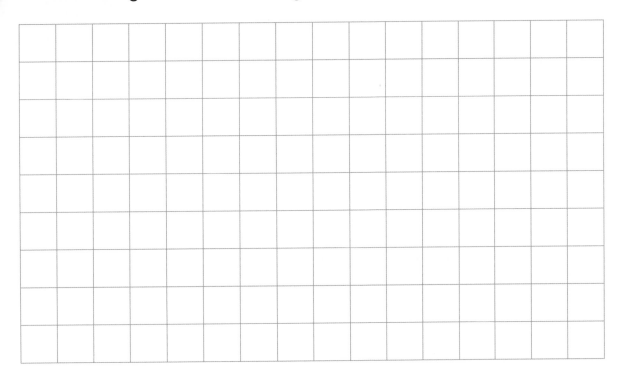

4 It is impossible to draw a triangle with 2 obtuse angles.
Show why this is impossible on the grid below.

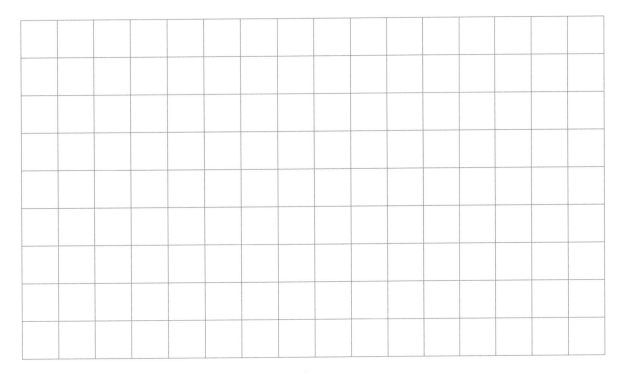

Geometry: perimeter

Starter

Jacob cuts out a rectangle from a larger rectangle.

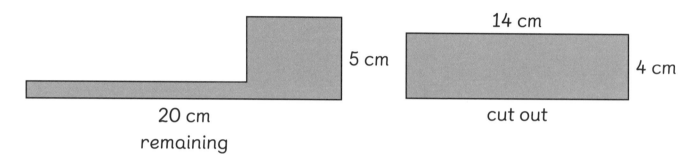

20 cm remaining

14 cm

5 cm

4 cm

cut out

What is the perimeter of the remaining shape?

Example

Start by working out the length of each side of the remaining shape.

14 cm

4 cm

cut out

20 − 14 = 6

5 − 4 = 1

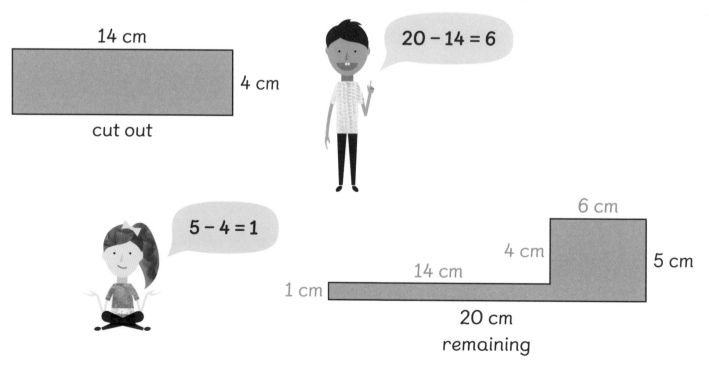

6 cm

4 cm

14 cm

1 cm

5 cm

20 cm remaining

Add the lengths of the sides of the remaining shape.
The perimeter of the remaining shape is 50 cm.

1 Oak cuts a piece from a square cake.
Find the perimeter of the remaining shape.

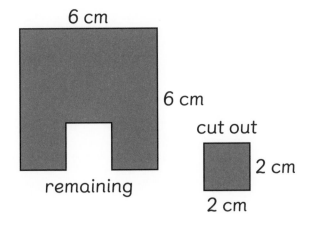

The perimeter of the remaining shape is [   ] .

2 A carpenter cuts two pieces from a rectangle of wood.
Find the perimeter of the remaining shape.

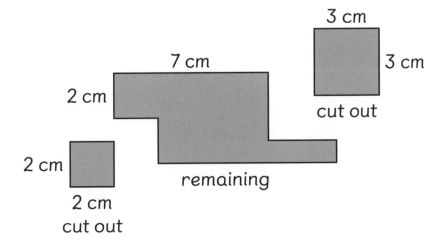

The perimeter of the remaining shape is [   ] .

Answers

Page 5 **1 (a)** 874 **(b)** 134 **(c)** 873 **(d)** 137 **2** 134, 137, 873, 874 **3 (a–b)** 963, 936, 693, 639, 396, 369

Page 7 **1 (a)** 487, 497, 507, 517, 527 **(b)** 45, 145, 245, 345, 445, 545 **(c)** 909, 809, 709, 609, 509, 409 **2 (a)** 318, 328, 338, 348, 358, 368 **(b)** 761, 751, 741, 731, 721, 711 **(c)** 506, 406, 306, 206, 106, 6 **3** Answers will vary.

Page 9 **1 (a)** 656 + 37 = 693 **(b)** 319 + 88 = 407 **(c)** 486 + 75 = 561 **(d)** 524 + 96 = 620 **2 (a)** 132 + 389 = 521 **(b)** 465 + 456 = 921 **(c)** 725 + 188 = 913 **(d)** 333 + 599 = 932

Page 11 **1** The car park can hold 495 cars altogether. **2** Sam and Charles scored 641 points altogether.

Page 13 **1** The gardener has 273 bulbs left to plant. **2** There were 89 customers who came to the restaurant for dinner. **3** 237 children stayed on the field.

Page 15 **1** 563 − 478 = 85. The difference between the two distances is 85 m. **2** 801 − 78 = 723. The mass of the water buffalo is 723 kg.

Page 17 **1** 42 × 7 = 294. There are 294 rulers in the 7 classrooms altogether. **2** 24 × 9 = 216. The children buy 216 stickers altogether.

Page 18 **1** 70 ÷ 5 = 14. Each child gets 14 tennis balls.

Page 19 **2** 52 ÷ 4 = 13. They make 13 piles of books. **3** 3 × 28 = 84, 84 ÷ 6 = 14. The children plant 14 rows of seeds altogether.

Page 20 **1** Lulu has 30 books.

Page 21 **2** Bus A takes 54 children. Bus B takes 18 children. Bus C takes 28 children. **3** There are 168 crayons altogether.

Page 23 **1** $\frac{3}{7}$ of the chocolate bar is left. **2** $\frac{4}{9}$ of the puzzle hasn't been completed. **3** $\frac{3}{10}$ of the art paper is left.

Page 25 **1 (a)** $\frac{3}{9} = \frac{1}{3}$ **(b)** $\frac{6}{10} = \frac{3}{5}$ **(c)** $\frac{8}{12} = \frac{24}{36}$ **2 (a)** $\frac{1}{6} + \frac{3}{6} = \frac{4}{6}, \frac{6}{6} - \frac{4}{6} = \frac{2}{6} = \frac{1}{3}. \frac{1}{3}$ of the watermelon was left. **(b)** $\frac{1}{4}$ of the dozen was left .

Page 27 **1** $\frac{3}{4}$ is greater than $\frac{3}{5}$. **2** $\frac{4}{7}$ is less than $\frac{4}{5}$. **3 (a)** Charles **(b)** Ravi

Page 29 **1** Each child gets $\frac{5}{4}$ oranges. **2** Each child gets $\frac{4}{5}$ of a pie. **3** Each friend gets $\frac{7}{6}$ bars of chocolate.

Page 31　**1** 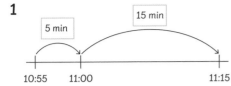 5 + 15 = 20. The morning break is 20 minutes long. **2** The programme was 38 minutes long. **3** Charles stopped reading his book at 8:28 p.m.

Page 33　**1 (a)** The class starts at 5 minutes to 10 in the morning. **(b)** The class starts at 15 minutes to 3 in the afternoon. We can write 14:45 as 2:45 p.m. **(c)** The class starts at 10 minutes past 5 in the afternoon. We can write 17:10 as 5:10 p.m. **2 (a)** 27 minutes past 10 in the morning **(b)** 9 minutes past 1 in the afternoon; 1:09 p.m.

Page 35　**1** 21 ÷ 7 = 3. Elliott uses 3 l of water each day. **2** The volume of juice in the box is 200 ml. **3** The capacity of the jug is 3 l.

Page 37　**1** Amira got £21 and 45p change. **2** Sam got £4 and 25p change.

Page 39　**1** The price of the hoodie is £24. The price of the shirt is £6. **2** The builder spends £16. The plumber spends £48. The electrician spends £96.

Page 41　**1**

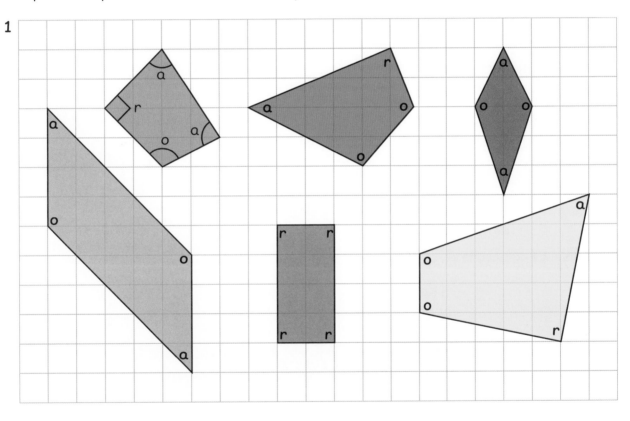

Answers continued

Page 42   2 (a) Answers will vary. For example:

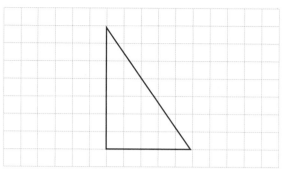

(b) Answers will vary. For example:

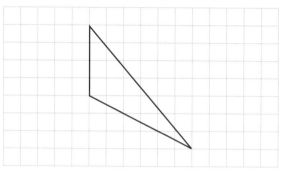

Page 43   3 Answers will vary. For example:

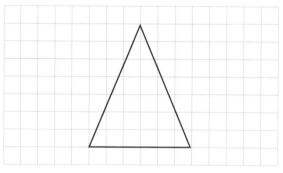

4 Answers will vary.

Page 45   1 The perimeter of the remaining shape is 28 cm. 2 The perimeter of the remaining shape is 28 cm.